My Invention Log

Invention Name: _____

Date Created: ___/___/___

Patent Obtained? Yes   No   In Progress

Notes/Features of Invention:

_____

_____

_____

_____

_____

_____

_____

_____

_____

_____

_____

_____

_____

_____

_____

_____

_____

_____

_____

Invention Name: _____

Date Created: ___/___/___

Patent Obtained? Yes   No   In Progress

Notes/Features of Invention:

_____

_____

_____

_____

_____

_____

_____

_____

_____

_____

_____

_____

_____

_____

_____

_____

_____

_____

_____

_____

Invention Name: _____

Date Created: ___/___/___

Patent Obtained? Yes   No   In Progress

Notes/Features of Invention:

_____

_____

_____

_____

_____

_____

_____

_____

_____

_____

_____

_____

_____

_____

_____

_____

_____

_____

_____

Invention Name: _____

Date Created: ___/___/___

Patent Obtained? Yes   No   In Progress

Notes/Features of Invention:

_____

_____

_____

_____

_____

_____

_____

_____

_____

_____

_____

_____

_____

_____

_____

_____

_____

_____

_____

Invention Name: _____

Date Created: ___/___/___

Patent Obtained? Yes   No   In Progress

Notes/Features of Invention:

_____

_____

_____

_____

_____

_____

_____

_____

_____

_____

_____

_____

_____

_____

_____

_____

_____

_____

_____

Invention Name: _____

Date Created: ___/___/___

Patent Obtained? Yes   No   In Progress

Notes/Features of Invention:

_____

_____

_____

_____

_____

_____

_____

_____

_____

_____

_____

_____

_____

_____

_____

_____

_____

_____

_____

_____

_____

Invention Name: _____

Date Created: ___/___/___

Patent Obtained? Yes   No   In Progress

Notes/Features of Invention:

_____

_____

_____

_____

_____

_____

_____

_____

_____

_____

_____

_____

_____

_____

_____

_____

_____

_____

_____

Invention Name: _____

Date Created: ___/___/___

Patent Obtained? Yes   No   In Progress

Notes/Features of Invention:

_____
_____
_____
_____
_____
_____
_____
_____
_____
_____
_____
_____
_____
_____
_____
_____
_____
_____
_____

Invention Name: _____

Date Created: ___/___/___

Patent Obtained? Yes   No   In Progress

Notes/Features of Invention:

_____

_____

_____

_____

_____

_____

_____

_____

_____

_____

_____

_____

_____

_____

_____

_____

_____

_____

_____

Invention Name: _____

Date Created: ____/____/____

Patent Obtained? Yes   No   In Progress

Notes/Features of Invention:

_____

_____

_____

_____

_____

_____

_____

_____

_____

_____

_____

_____

_____

_____

_____

_____

_____

_____

Invention Name: _____

Date Created: ___/___/___

Patent Obtained? Yes   No   In Progress

Notes/Features of Invention:

_____

_____

_____

_____

_____

_____

_____

_____

_____

_____

_____

_____

_____

_____

_____

_____

_____

_____

_____

_____

Invention Name: _____

Date Created: ___/___/___

Patent Obtained? Yes   No   In Progress

Notes/Features of Invention:

_____
_____
_____
_____
_____
_____
_____
_____
_____
_____
_____
_____
_____
_____
_____
_____
_____
_____
_____
_____

Invention Name: _____

Date Created: ___/___/___

Patent Obtained? Yes   No   In Progress

Notes/Features of Invention:

_____

_____

_____

_____

_____

_____

_____

_____

_____

_____

_____

_____

_____

_____

_____

_____

_____

_____

_____

Invention Name: _____

Date Created: ___/___/___

Patent Obtained? Yes   No   In Progress

Notes/Features of Invention:

_____

_____

_____

_____

_____

_____

_____

_____

_____

_____

_____

_____

_____

_____

_____

_____

_____

_____

_____

Invention Name: _____

Date Created: ___/___/___

Patent Obtained? Yes   No   In Progress

Notes/Features of Invention:

_____

_____

_____

_____

_____

_____

_____

_____

_____

_____

_____

_____

_____

_____

_____

_____

_____

_____

_____

_____

Invention Name: _____

Date Created: ____/____/____

Patent Obtained? Yes   No   In Progress

Notes/Features of Invention:

_____

_____

_____

_____

_____

_____

_____

_____

_____

_____

_____

_____

_____

_____

_____

_____

_____

_____

_____

Invention Name: _____

Date Created: ___/___/___

Patent Obtained? Yes   No   In Progress

Notes/Features of Invention:

_____

_____

_____

_____

_____

_____

_____

_____

_____

_____

_____

_____

_____

_____

_____

_____

_____

_____

_____

Invention Name: _____

Date Created: ___/___/___

Patent Obtained? Yes   No   In Progress

Notes/Features of Invention:

_____

_____

_____

_____

_____

_____

_____

_____

_____

_____

_____

_____

_____

_____

_____

_____

_____

_____

_____

_____

Invention Name: _____

Date Created: ____/____/____

Patent Obtained? Yes   No   In Progress

Notes/Features of Invention:

_____

_____

_____

_____

_____

_____

_____

_____

_____

_____

_____

_____

_____

_____

_____

_____

_____

_____

Invention Name: _____

Date Created: ___/___/___

Patent Obtained? Yes   No   In Progress

Notes/Features of Invention:

_____

_____

_____

_____

_____

_____

_____

_____

_____

_____

_____

_____

_____

_____

_____

_____

_____

_____

_____

Invention Name: _____

Date Created: ___/___/___

Patent Obtained? Yes   No   In Progress

Notes/Features of Invention:

_____

_____

_____

_____

_____

_____

_____

_____

_____

_____

_____

_____

_____

_____

_____

_____

_____

_____

_____

_____

Invention Name: _____
Date Created: ___/___/___
Patent Obtained? Yes   No   In Progress

Notes/Features of Invention:

_____
_____
_____
_____
_____
_____
_____
_____
_____
_____
_____
_____
_____
_____
_____
_____
_____
_____
_____

Invention Name: _____

Date Created: ___/___/___

Patent Obtained? Yes   No   In Progress

Notes/Features of Invention:

_____

_____

_____

_____

_____

_____

_____

_____

_____

_____

_____

_____

_____

_____

_____

_____

_____

_____

Invention Name: _____

Date Created: ___ / ___ / ___

Patent Obtained? Yes   No   In Progress

Notes/Features of Invention:

_____

_____

_____

_____

_____

_____

_____

_____

_____

_____

_____

_____

_____

_____

_____

_____

_____

_____

Invention Name: _____

Date Created: ___/___/___

Patent Obtained? Yes   No   In Progress

Notes/Features of Invention:

_____
_____
_____
_____
_____
_____
_____
_____
_____
_____
_____
_____
_____
_____
_____
_____
_____
_____
_____
_____
_____
_____

Invention Name: _____

Date Created: ___/___/___

Patent Obtained? Yes   No   In Progress

Notes/Features of Invention:

_____

_____

_____

_____

_____

_____

_____

_____

_____

_____

_____

_____

_____

_____

_____

_____

_____

_____

_____

_____

Invention Name: _____

Date Created: ___/___/___

Patent Obtained? Yes   No   In Progress

Notes/Features of Invention:

_____

_____

_____

_____

_____

_____

_____

_____

_____

_____

_____

_____

_____

_____

_____

_____

_____

_____

_____

_____

Invention Name: _____

Date Created: ___/___/___

Patent Obtained? Yes   No   In Progress

Notes/Features of Invention:

_____

_____

_____

_____

_____

_____

_____

_____

_____

_____

_____

_____

_____

_____

_____

_____

_____

_____

_____

Invention Name: _____

Date Created: ___ / ___ / ___

Patent Obtained? Yes   No   In Progress

Notes/Features of Invention:

_____
_____
_____
_____
_____
_____
_____
_____
_____
_____
_____
_____
_____
_____
_____
_____
_____
_____
_____

Invention Name: _____

Date Created: ___ / ___ / ___

Patent Obtained? Yes   No   In Progress

Notes/Features of Invention:

_____

_____

_____

_____

_____

_____

_____

_____

_____

_____

_____

_____

_____

_____

_____

_____

_____

_____

_____

Invention Name: _____

Date Created: ___/___/___

Patent Obtained? Yes   No   In Progress

Notes/Features of Invention:

_____

_____

_____

_____

_____

_____

_____

_____

_____

_____

_____

_____

_____

_____

_____

_____

_____

_____

_____

Invention Name: _____

Date Created: ___/___/___

Patent Obtained? Yes   No   In Progress

Notes/Features of Invention:

_____

_____

_____

_____

_____

_____

_____

_____

_____

_____

_____

_____

_____

_____

_____

_____

_____

_____

Invention Name: _____

Date Created: ___/___/___

Patent Obtained? Yes   No   In Progress

Notes/Features of Invention:

_____

_____

_____

_____

_____

_____

_____

_____

_____

_____

_____

_____

_____

_____

_____

_____

_____

_____

_____

_____

Invention Name: _____

Date Created: ___/___/___

Patent Obtained? Yes   No   In Progress

Notes/Features of Invention:

_____

_____

_____

_____

_____

_____

_____

_____

_____

_____

_____

_____

_____

_____

_____

_____

_____

_____

_____

Invention Name: _____

Date Created: ___/___/___

Patent Obtained? Yes   No   In Progress

Notes/Features of Invention:

_____

_____

_____

_____

_____

_____

_____

_____

_____

_____

_____

_____

_____

_____

_____

_____

_____

_____

_____

Invention Name: _____

Date Created: ___/___/___

Patent Obtained? Yes   No   In Progress

Notes/Features of Invention:

_____

_____

_____

_____

_____

_____

_____

_____

_____

_____

_____

_____

_____

_____

_____

_____

_____

_____

_____

_____

_____

Invention Name: _____

Date Created: ___/___/___

Patent Obtained? Yes   No   In Progress

Notes/Features of Invention:

_____

_____

_____

_____

_____

_____

_____

_____

_____

_____

_____

_____

_____

_____

_____

_____

_____

_____

_____

_____

_____

Invention Name: _____

Date Created: ___/___/___

Patent Obtained? Yes   No   In Progress

Notes/Features of Invention:

_____

_____

_____

_____

_____

_____

_____

_____

_____

_____

_____

_____

_____

_____

_____

_____

_____

_____

_____

Invention Name: _____

Date Created: ___/___/___

Patent Obtained? Yes   No   In Progress

Notes/Features of Invention:

_____

_____

_____

_____

_____

_____

_____

_____

_____

_____

_____

_____

_____

_____

_____

_____

_____

_____

_____

Invention Name: _____

Date Created: ____/____/____

Patent Obtained? Yes   No   In Progress

Notes/Features of Invention:

_____

_____

_____

_____

_____

_____

_____

_____

_____

_____

_____

_____

_____

_____

_____

_____

_____

_____

_____

_____

Invention Name: _____

Date Created: ___/___/___

Patent Obtained? Yes   No   In Progress

Notes/Features of Invention:

_____

_____

_____

_____

_____

_____

_____

_____

_____

_____

_____

_____

_____

_____

_____

_____

_____

_____

_____

_____

Invention Name: _____

Date Created: ___/___/___

Patent Obtained? Yes   No   In Progress

Notes/Features of Invention:

_____

_____

_____

_____

_____

_____

_____

_____

_____

_____

_____

_____

_____

_____

_____

_____

_____

_____

_____

_____

Invention Name: _____

Date Created: ___/___/___

Patent Obtained? Yes   No   In Progress

Notes/Features of Invention:

_____

_____

_____

_____

_____

_____

_____

_____

_____

_____

_____

_____

_____

_____

_____

_____

_____

_____

_____

Invention Name: _____

Date Created: ___/___/___

Patent Obtained? Yes   No   In Progress

Notes/Features of Invention:

_____

_____

_____

_____

_____

_____

_____

_____

_____

_____

_____

_____

_____

_____

_____

_____

_____

_____

_____

_____

_____

Invention Name: _____

Date Created: ___/___/___

Patent Obtained? Yes   No   In Progress

Notes/Features of Invention:

_____

_____

_____

_____

_____

_____

_____

_____

_____

_____

_____

_____

_____

_____

_____

_____

_____

_____

Invention Name: _____

Date Created: ___/___/___

Patent Obtained? Yes   No   In Progress

Notes/Features of Invention:

_____

_____

_____

_____

_____

_____

_____

_____

_____

_____

_____

_____

_____

_____

_____

_____

_____

_____

_____

Invention Name: _____

Date Created: ___/___/___

Patent Obtained? Yes   No   In Progress

Notes/Features of Invention:

_____

_____

_____

_____

_____

_____

_____

_____

_____

_____

_____

_____

_____

_____

_____

_____

_____

_____

Invention Name: _____

Date Created: ____/____/____

Patent Obtained? Yes   No   In Progress

Notes/Features of Invention:

_____

_____

_____

_____

_____

_____

_____

_____

_____

_____

_____

_____

_____

_____

_____

_____

_____

_____

_____

Invention Name: _____

Date Created: ____/____/____

Patent Obtained? Yes   No   In Progress

Notes/Features of Invention:

_____

_____

_____

_____

_____

_____

_____

_____

_____

_____

_____

_____

_____

_____

_____

_____

_____

_____

_____

_____

Invention Name: _____

Date Created: ___/___/___

Patent Obtained? Yes   No   In Progress

Notes/Features of Invention:

_____

_____

_____

_____

_____

_____

_____

_____

_____

_____

_____

_____

_____

_____

_____

_____

_____

_____

_____

Invention Name: _____

Date Created: ___/___/___

Patent Obtained? Yes   No   In Progress

Notes/Features of Invention:

_____

_____

_____

_____

_____

_____

_____

_____

_____

_____

_____

_____

_____

_____

_____

_____

_____

_____

_____

Invention Name: _____

Date Created: ___ / ___ / ___

Patent Obtained? Yes   No   In Progress

Notes/Features of Invention:

_____
_____
_____
_____
_____
_____
_____
_____
_____
_____
_____
_____
_____
_____
_____
_____
_____
_____
_____

Invention Name: _____

Date Created: ___/___/___

Patent Obtained? Yes   No   In Progress

Notes/Features of Invention:

_____

_____

_____

_____

_____

_____

_____

_____

_____

_____

_____

_____

_____

_____

_____

_____

_____

_____

_____

Invention Name: _____

Date Created: ____/____/____

Patent Obtained? Yes   No   In Progress

Notes/Features of Invention:

_____

_____

_____

_____

_____

_____

_____

_____

_____

_____

_____

_____

_____

_____

_____

_____

_____

_____

_____

Invention Name: _____

Date Created: ___/___/___

Patent Obtained? Yes   No   In Progress

Notes/Features of Invention:

_____

_____

_____

_____

_____

_____

_____

_____

_____

_____

_____

_____

_____

_____

_____

_____

_____

_____

_____

Invention Name: _____

Date Created: ___/___/___

Patent Obtained? Yes   No   In Progress

Notes/Features of Invention:

_____

_____

_____

_____

_____

_____

_____

_____

_____

_____

_____

_____

_____

_____

_____

_____

_____

_____

_____

Invention Name: _____

Date Created: ___/___/___

Patent Obtained? Yes   No   In Progress

Notes/Features of Invention:

_____

_____

_____

_____

_____

_____

_____

_____

_____

_____

_____

_____

_____

_____

_____

_____

_____

_____

_____

Invention Name: _____

Date Created: ___/___/___

Patent Obtained? Yes   No   In Progress

Notes/Features of Invention:

_____

_____

_____

_____

_____

_____

_____

_____

_____

_____

_____

_____

_____

_____

_____

_____

_____

_____

Invention Name: _____

Date Created: ___/___/___

Patent Obtained? Yes   No   In Progress

Notes/Features of Invention:

_____

_____

_____

_____

_____

_____

_____

_____

_____

_____

_____

_____

_____

_____

_____

_____

_____

_____

_____

_____

Invention Name: _____

Date Created: ___/___/___

Patent Obtained? Yes   No   In Progress

Notes/Features of Invention:

_____

_____

_____

_____

_____

_____

_____

_____

_____

_____

_____

_____

_____

_____

_____

_____

_____

_____

_____

Invention Name: _____

Date Created: ___/___/___

Patent Obtained? Yes   No   In Progress

Notes/Features of Invention:

_____

_____

_____

_____

_____

_____

_____

_____

_____

_____

_____

_____

_____

_____

_____

_____

_____

_____